The Pledge of Allegiance

by Pamela Dell

Content Adviser: Kathryn V. Kingsbury,
Elementary school teacher, Hershey, Pennsylvania

Reading Adviser: Dr. Linda D. Labbo, Department of Reading Education,
College of Education, The University of Georgia

Let's See Library
Compass Point Books
Minneapolis, Minnesota

Compass Point Books
3109 West 50th Street, #115
Minneapolis, MN 55410

Visit Compass Point Books on the Internet at *www.compasspointbooks.com* or e-mail your
request to *custserv@compasspointbooks.com*

On the cover: Third graders at a Starkville, Mississippi, elementary school recite the Pledge of Allegiance.

Photographs ©: AP Wide World/Starkville Daily News, Brian Loden, cover; Underwood & Underwood/Corbis, 4;
Brooks Kraft/Corbis, 6; Bettmann/Corbis, 8, 16; Hulton/Archive by Getty Images, 10; Lee Snider/Corbis, 12;
Courtesy of the President Benjamin Harrison Home, Indianapolis, 14; Corbis, 18; AFP/Corbis, 20.

Editor: Catherine Neitge
Photo Researcher: Marcie C. Spence
Designers/Page Production: Melissa Kes and Jaime Martens/Les Tranby

Library of Congress Cataloging-in-Publication Data
Dell, Pamela.
    The Pledge of Allegiance / by Pamela Dell.
        p. cm. — (Let's see)
Summary: Describes the history of the Pledge of Allegiance and the changes that have been made to it since it
was first written in 1892.
Includes bibliographical references and index.
ISBN 0-7565-0620-4 (hardcover)
1. Bellamy, Francis. Pledge of Allegiance to the Flag—Juvenile literature. 2. Flags—United States—Juvenile
literature. [1. Pledge of Allegiance.] I. Title. II. Series.
    JC346.D45 2004
    323.6'5'0973—dc22   2003014460

Table of Contents

What Is a Pledge of Allegiance? 5

What Are the Words of the Pledge of Allegiance? 7

How Did the Pledge Get Started? 9

Did Schools Always Fly Flags? 11

Why Was the Pledge Written? 13

When Did Americans Begin Saying the Pledge? 15

How Has the Pledge Changed? 17

What Is the Correct Way to Say the Pledge? 19

Was the Pledge Meant Only for Children? 21

Glossary 22

Did You Know? 22

Want to Know More? 23

Index 24

NOTE: In this book, words that are defined in the glossary
are in **bold** the first time they appear in the text.

What Is a Pledge of Allegiance?

American children first learned to **salute** the flag more than 100 years ago. Along with the salute, the children would recite 23 words that were called the Pledge of Allegiance. They were taught this pledge at school.

A pledge is a promise. Allegiance means to be faithful, loyal, or true. A pledge of allegiance means a promise to always be faithful to someone or something.

When Americans say the Pledge of Allegiance, they are promising to be true to their country. They are making a pledge to always be loyal citizens. Their words mean they are proud of their country.

◀ *The way children salute the flag has changed, but the meaning remains the same.*

What Are the Words of the Pledge of Allegiance?

The original 23 words of the Pledge of Allegiance grew to 31 words in 1954. Those words have stayed the same ever since. They are:

> *I pledge allegiance to the flag*
> *of the United States of America,*
> *And to the Republic for which it stands:*
> *One nation under God,* **indivisible,**
> *with* **liberty** *and* **justice** *for all.*

Pledging to the flag also means believing in the United States as a republic. In a republic, the people are in charge. They choose their leaders to run the government.

◄ *President George W. Bush recites the Pledge of Allegiance with Tennessee schoolchildren.*

How Did the Pledge Get Started?

The Pledge of Allegiance came about because of two men in the late 1880s. Their names were James Upham and Francis Bellamy. They lived near Boston, Massachusetts, where they worked for the Perry Mason Company. This company owned a children's magazine called The Youth's Companion.

Upham and Bellamy shared a deep love of the United States. They felt children should be taught to love their country, too. They believed children would become more **patriotic** if they learned about the American flag at school.

◄ *Children salute the flag in the early 1890s. That's when they started learning about the flag at school.*

Did Schools Always Fly Flags?

Between 1888 and 1892, an important change was made in American schools. James Upham believed all schools in the United States should fly the American flag. At that time, few schools in the country had flags.

Upham worked hard to make this change happen. Soon, American educators began to agree with this new idea. Today, the American flag can be found in every school in the United States. This is because of James Upham.

He also felt it was important to salute the flag. He wanted to write a pledge that children could say together every day in class.

◀ *Schoolchildren recite the Pledge of Allegiance in 1935.*

Why Was the Pledge Written?

In 1892, The Youth's Companion began planning a big Columbus Day program. Christopher Columbus had first come to North America 400 years earlier. He had sailed west from Europe looking for new lands.

The Columbus Day program was called the National Public School Celebration. It was a special eight-part program that all U.S. classrooms could use.

Upham and Bellamy were in charge of planning this very first Columbus Day celebration. Upham wanted to write a Pledge of Allegiance for the program. He tried writing the pledge himself. He did not like what he wrote. Finally, he asked Bellamy to write the pledge, and Bellamy agreed.

◀ *A monument to Christopher Columbus was erected in New York City in 1892.*

When Did Americans Begin Saying the Pledge?

Francis Bellamy wrote the Pledge of Allegiance, but James Upham had the final **approval.** After many changes, the pledge was ready to be printed.

The Pledge of Allegiance was printed for the first time on September 8, 1892. It appeared in The Youth's Companion.

President Benjamin Harrison issued a **proclamation** asking schools to take part in activities honoring Christopher Columbus. So, on October 21, 1892, Columbus Day was celebrated all over the country. Teachers used the Pledge of Allegiance as part of their classroom celebrations.

◀ *President Benjamin Harrison (center) urged schools to honor Columbus in 1892.*

How Has the Pledge Changed?

The Pledge of Allegiance written by Francis Bellamy was:

> *I pledge allegiance to my Flag,*
> *and to the Republic for which it stands:*
> *One Nation indivisible,*
> *With Liberty and Justice for all.*

The pledge to the flag was first changed in 1923 and then in 1924. The words "my Flag" were dropped. The words "the flag of the United States of America" were added. That was to make sure everyone was thinking about the U.S. flag.

In 1954, the words "under God" were added. That was the last change made to the pledge.

◄ President Eisenhower (in long coat, third from right) recites the Pledge of Allegiance at a 1956 baseball game. He was president when the pledge was last changed.

What Is the Correct Way to Say the Pledge of Allegiance?

In 1892, children were taught to give a military salute at the beginning of the pledge. They saluted until the words "to my flag" were spoken. Then they would stretch their right arm out toward the flag. At the end of the pledge, they dropped their arm. This method changed in 1942.

Today, people still stand and face the flag while saying the pledge. Now, however, people hold their right hand over their heart while saying the words. One important thing has not changed. They are still showing their loyalty to the United States.

◀ *California schoolchildren recite the Pledge of Allegiance in 1942, the year the method of salute changed.*

Was the Pledge of Allegiance Meant Only for Children?

The Pledge of Allegiance was written for children. The authors believed it was for everyone, however. Francis Bellamy and James Upham wanted people to say the pledge whenever the American flag was raised.

When the Pledge of Allegiance was 50 years old, Congress made the pledge official. There are special laws about handling the flag. The laws are called the Flag Code. Congress added the pledge to these laws in 1942.

Now the pledge is more than 110 years old. In just a few words, it lets Americans show their love for a country that offers liberty and justice for all.

◀ *Children across the United States, including these students in Washington, D.C., recited the pledge together on October 12, 2001. It has become a yearly event.*

Glossary

approval—to allow
indivisible—unable to be broken apart or divided into separate pieces
liberty—freedom
justice—fair treatment

patriotic—to show loyal support for one's country
proclamation—an official announcement
salute—to show respect by raising the right hand to the forehead

Did You Know?

• Some people think the Pledge of Allegiance should be banned from public schools for its use of the words "under God." They think the pledge has become a public prayer. A lawsuit about the pledge has made its way to the Supreme Court. The court has already ruled that students cannot be required to recite the pledge.

• The way people salute the flag was changed in 1942 because it looked too much like the German Nazi salute. The United States was in the middle of a war with Germany at the time.

• Erle Stanley Gardner was a famous mystery writer. He read The Youth's Companion as a child. Later, he named the main character in his books Perry Mason after the publishing company's name.

• Francis Bellamy could not put his name on the Pledge of Allegiance because his magazine did not name its writers. Some people still think James Upham wrote it.

• The first time adults recited the pledge together was on April 25, 1893. They were attending a flag-raising ceremony at a lighthouse in New Jersey. It was called the Navesink Light Station. Today, it is known as the Twin Lights Historic Site.

• Through the years, Columbus Day has been celebrated on different days. In 1892, President Benjamin Harrison proclaimed October 21 as Columbus Day. In 1937, President Franklin D. Roosevelt proclaimed October 12 as Columbus Day. In 1971, Columbus Day was changed to the second Monday of October.

Want to Know More?

In the Library

Bellamy, Francis. *The Pledge of Allegiance.*
New York: Cartwheel Books, 2001.
Cheney, Lynne V. *America: A Patriotic Primer.*
New York: Simon & Schuster, 2002.
Sampson, Michael, and Bill Martin Jr.
I Pledge Allegiance. Boston: Candlewick
Press, 2002.

On the Web

For more information on the *Pledge of Allegiance,* use FactHound to track down Web sites related to this book.

1. Go to *www.compasspointbooks. com/facthound*
2. Type in this book ID: 0756506204
3. Click on the *Fetch It* button.

Your trusty FactHound will fetch the best Web sites for you!

Through the Mail

Celebration U.S.A.
17853 Santiago Blvd., Suite 107
Villa Park, CA 92861
714/283-1892
To learn about Pledge Across America, in which schoolchildren across the United States recite the pledge at the same time on the same day

On the Road

Navesink Twin Lights
Twin Lights Historic Site
Lighthouse Road
Highlands, NJ 07732
732/872-1814
To visit the lighthouse where the Pledge of Allegiance was recited in 1893

Index

allegiance, 5
Bellamy, Francis, 9, 13, 15, 17, 21
Bush, George W., *6*
changes, 17
children, *4,* 5, *6, 8,* 9, *10,* 11, *18,* 19, *20,* 21
Columbus, Christopher, *12,* 13, 15
Columbus Day, 13, 15
Congress, 21
Eisenhower, Dwight D., *16*
flag, *4,* 5, *6,* 7, *8,* 9, *10,* 11, 17, 19, *20,* 21
Flag Code, 21
government, 7

Harrison, Benjamin, *14,* 15
military salutes, 19
National Public School Celebration, 13
patriotism, 9
Perry Mason Company, 9
proclamation, 15
salutes, *4,* 5, *6, 8, 10,* 11, *16, 18,* 19, *20*
schools, *4,* 5, *8,* 9, *10,* 11, 15
teachers, *4, 8,* 15, *20*
Upham, James, 9, 11, 13, 15, 21
The Youth's Companion magazine, 9, 13, 15

About the Author

Pamela Dell was born in Idaho, grew up in Chicago, and now lives in Southern California. She began her professional career writing for adults and started writing for children about 12 years ago. Since then she has published fiction and nonfiction books, written numerous magazine articles, and created award-winning interactive multimedia. Among many other things, Pamela loves technology, the Internet, books, movies, curious people, and cats, especially black cats.

4.8 AR Book Level
0.5 pts.